George Warren in association with **Park Theatre**
presents

D0555661

Fishskin Trousers

by Elizabeth Kuti

Fishskin Trousers opened at Park Theatre, London, on
17 October 2017

The play was first performed at the Finborough Theatre, London,
on 3 September 2013

Fishskin Trousers

by Elizabeth Kuti

Cast

MAB	Jessica Carroll
BEN	Brett Brown
MOG	Eva Traynor

Creative Team

Director	Robert Price
Lighting Designer	Matt Leventhall
Designer	Nancy Surman

Creative Team

Elizabeth Kuti | Writer

Elizabeth Kuti started her career as an actor in Irish theatre and her roles included the Colleen Bawn in *The Colleen Bawn* (Lyttelton, National Theatre and Abbey Theatre, Dublin).

Writing for theatre includes: *The Sugar Wife* (Soho Theatre, 2006; winner of the Susan Smith Blackburn Award 2006; Irish Times Best New Play nomination); *The Whisperers* (Traverse Theatre, Edinburgh, 1999/Irish tour); *The Six-Days World* (attachment at National Theatre Studio; Finborough Theatre, London, 2007); *Treehouses* (winner of the Stewart Parker radio award; *Peacock* (Abbey Theatre, Dublin, 2000/Northcott Theatre Exeter, 2001). For the Miniaturists, short plays include: *Time Spent on Trains* (Southwark Playhouse); *Eighty Miles* (Southwark Playhouse); *Enter A Gentleman* (Arcola Theatre/National Portrait Gallery, London).

Most recently, she has been Playwright-in-Residence at Hampton Court Palace (2015–6). In 2015 her collection of micro-dramas, *TimePlays*, was seen by 400,000 visitors at Hampton Court; and in 2016 the Palace staged *Encounters from the Past* (directed by Jo McInnes) and *Elizabethan Christmas*.

Other recent writing for theatre includes: *Cold Season in Calcutta* (directed by Trilby James, reading at the Mercury Theatre, 2017); *Blue Pencil* for LAMDA (directed by Robert Price, long project 2017); *United Incandescent*, commissioned by the National Theatre (rehearsed reading at the Old Red Lion Theatre, London, in September 2015; and at the Vanburgh Theatre, London, in August 2014); *Fishskin Trousers* (which has received productions in London, Canada and Greece, 2013–15).

Recent radio drama includes: *Reader I Mended Him* (BBC Radio 4, 2016); *Sitters' Stories* (BBC Radio 4, 2015); *Dear Mr Spectator* (comedy-drama adaptation of Addison and Steele's *Spectator* papers) – two series, broadcast on Woman's Hour, Radio 4 in 2009 and 2010; *May Child* (starring Patricia Routledge); *The Glasswright* (starring Tim McInerny) both for BBC Radio 4; and for BBC Radio 3, a ninety-minute drama, *Mr Fielding's Scandal-Shop* (broadcast Christmas Day, 2005, starring Ron Cook).

Elizabeth teaches drama and playwriting at the University of Essex; and is a long-term collaborator with director Robert Price with whom she founded Lubkinfinds Theatre.

Robert Price | Director

Robert Price currently works at LAMDA in West London as a director and voice teacher having previously held the senior post in voice and text at RADA. He has also taught and directed at RCSSD, Arts Ed, East 15, The University of Essex, The Lir in Dublin, Trinity College Dublin and for BADA in Oxford.

Before working as a teacher Robert was an actor in Dublin playing with most of the country's theatre companies including productions with Bedrock, Loose Canon, The Corn Exchange, Rough Magic, Fishamble, Second Age, The Abbey and Peacock Theatres and The Gate. He is Artistic Director of Lubkinfinds Theatre Company together with his wife Elizabeth Kuti (who he met whilst working on the Dublin Fringe) and together they have developed and produced several new plays, short plays and readings including: *Fishskin Trousers*, *The Broken Token*, *Enter A Gentleman*, *Time Spent on Trains*, *Eighty Miles*, *United Incandescent* and *Blue Pencil* (as a LAMDA long project). Outside of his work with Lubkinfinds Robert has also directed new scripts by Glyn Maxwell, Philip Terry, Jonathan Lichenstein and Annecy Lax.

Matt Leventhall | Lighting Designer

Matt is the Head of Production Lighting at RADA.

Recent credits include: *Hamlet* (Kenneth Branagh Theatre Company, Associate to Paul Pyant); *The Terrible Infants* (Wilton's Music Hall); *Under The Market Roof* (Junction 8 Theatre, site specific/Mercury Theatre, Colchester); *Light* (Barbican/ Bristol Old Vic/ European tour); *Barbarians* (Young Vic); *The Comedy About a Bank Robbery* (Criterion, Associate LD); *My Mother Never Said I Should* (St James Theatre, Associate LD); *This Much* (*Or an Act of Violence Against The Institution of Marriage*) (Soho Theatre); *The Lizzie Play*, *All's Well That Ends Well* (GBS Theatre); *The Collector* (The Vaults Theatre); *The Vaudevillans* (Assembly); *Moth* (Hope Mill, Manchester); *Captain Flinn and the Pirate Dinosaurs 2: The Magic Cutlass* (Pleasance Theatre/UK tour); *hamlet is dead. no gravity*, *Ant Street* (Arcola Theatre); *Lady Anna All At Sea* (Park Theatre); *Animals* (Theatre503, Associate LD); *Tomcat* (Southwark *Playhouse*, Associate LD); *Scarlet* (Southwark Playhouse); *Islands* (New Diorama, Underbelly); *Divas* (Rose Theatre Kingston/Pleasance); *Poppies* (Space Theatre); *After Penelope, Pieces of Eight, Random, Mrs Warren's Profession, The Broken Token* (Gielgud Theatre); *A Christmas Carol, Bear* (Old Red Lion Theatre); *God's Own Country* (Zoo); *Sikes and Nancy* (Trafalgar Studios/UK tour); *Suffolk Stories* (Theatre Royal Bury St Edmunds); *Who Framed Roger Rabbit?* (Secret Cinema, site specific); *Yerma, Love For Love, High Society, In the Summer House* (Vanbrugh Theatre, RADA); *Have a Nice Life, But Not As We Know It, The Walworth Farce, Women of Troy, Land Without Words, The Cagebirds, Joseph K* (LAMDA Linbury); *Fishskin Trousers* (Finborough Theatre); *The Infant* (Vivien Cox Theatre); *Wild West End, Fresher The Musical* (Pleasance Theatre); *Bed* (Lakeside Arts Nottingham); *Madame Butterfly* (Leatherhead Theatre/UK tour); *Plug in the Lead, Mashup* (Leicester Square Theatre);*The Songs of My Life* (Garrick Theatre); TEDx London (The Roundhouse).

Up coming: *The Secret Garden* (Theatre by the Lake).

For a full list of credits and news visit www.mllx.co.uk

Nancy Surman | Designer

Nancy has been involved with a wide variety of productions including No 1 tours of *Dad's Army* and *'Allo 'Allo*, an outdoor production of *Animal Farm* in an old prison yard and the world premiere of *The Rinse Cycle* for Unexpected Opera, a shrunk adaptation of Wagner's 'Ring Cycle' set in a launderette!

Nancy's recent work includes: *Muswell Hill, African Gothic* (Park Theatre); *My Children, My Africa!* (Trafalgar Studios); *They're Playing Our Song* (Queen's Theatre, Hornchurch); *The Daughter-in-Law, Dangerous Corner* (New Vic Theatre, Stoke); *Can't Pay? Won't Pay!* (Oldham Coliseum).

International work includes: a Far East tour of Noël Coward's *Private Lives* and Shakespeare's *Much Ado about Nothing* in Vienna.

Other productions include: designs for *The Swing of Things* (Stephan Joseph Theatre, Scarborough); *A Stinging Sea* (Glasgow Citizens Theatre); *To Kill a Mockingbird, The Duchess of Malfi, The Rivals, The Winter's Tale* (Salisbury Playhouse); *The Accrington Pals* (Dukes Theatre, Lancaster); and Sondheim's *Into the Wood*s – twice!

Nancy designed Maxim Gorky's *Barbarians* (Salisbury Playhouse) for which she was nominated for the TMA Best Designer Award 2003.

Cast

Jessica Carroll | MAB
Trained at LAMDA.

Theatre includes: *The Broken Token* (Theatre Royal Bury St Edmunds, Lakeside/William Andrews Clark, Los Angeles); *Fishskin Trousers* (Finborough Theatre/Theatre Royal Bury St Edmunds, Lakeside); *Quirks* (Southwark Playhouse); *A Short History of the Royal Court* (Shoreditch Town Hall); *Old Bag* (Theatre503); *Climate Change Play in a Day* (Arcola Theatre); *Ghosts* (Battersea Arts Centre); *Hellcab* (Old Red Lion Theatre); *Last Seen* (Almeida Theatre); *A Woman of No Importance, Taking Steps* (Assembly Rooms Ludlow); *Daisy Pulls It Off* (Lyric Hammersmith).

Film includes: *Polar*.

Television includes: *Downton Abbey*.

Web series includes: *The Tone* and *Heads & Tails*.

Radio includes: *Life Begins at Crawley* and *The Future of Radio* (Radio 4) as well as being named 'highly commended' in the Carleton Hobbs BBC Radio Drama Competition.

Jessica has an extensive voiceover career in videogames, audiobooks, cartoons and the TV and film ADR circuit.

Brett Brown | BEN
Trained at RADA.

Theatre includes: his solo *Henry V [Man and Monarch]* (York Theatre Royal/international tour); *Hamlet* (HamletScenen, Kronborg Castle, Denmark); *Hamlet* (Gangdong Art Center, Korea); *The Tempest* (Royal Shakespeare Company); *Dear World* (Charing Cross Theatre); *Fishskin Trousers* (Finborough Theatre/Theatre Royal Bury St Edmunds); *Read Not Dead, Albertus Wallenstein, Perkin Warbeck* (Shakespeare's Globe); *Tiresias* (Bloomsbury Festival); *Macbeth* (Little Angel Theatre); *Dream On – Shakespeare's Dreams* (Ostrava Shakespeare Festival); *Phaedra* (The Cockpit); *Coalition: Westminster Side Story* (Theatre503); *Oh! What a Lovely War* (Haymarket Basingstoke); *The Tempest* (Gdansk Shakespeare Festival); *Last Seen* (Almeida Theatre).

Radio includes *The Cook and the Insurgent* (BBC).

Film includes *The Theory of Everything* (Working Title).

A distinguished singer, opera includes *Cavalleria Rusticana, Pagliacci, A Midsummer Night's Dream* (Opera Australia); *La Bohème* (OperaUpClose). Solo recitals include *Brett Brown sings Handel*, Bach's *Ich Habe Genug, Vivaldi: Lovers and Warriors, Postcards, To Sleep Perchance to Dream*.

Eva Traynor | MOG

Trained at RADA.

Theatre includes: *Hamlet* (East Riding Theatre); *A Midsummer Night's Dream, Pride and Prejudice, The Merchant of Venice, Arabian Nights* (RADA Cunard); *Fishskin Trousers* (Finborough Theatre/tour); *The Sea Plays* (Old Vic Tunnels)

Film/TV includes: *Queen of the Desert* (Werner Herzog); *Cheerful Weather for the Wedding* (Donald Rice/Goldcrest Films); *Shades of Love* (Gate Television); *The Rise of the Nazi Party* (WMR for Discovery Channel).

Radio includes: *Voices from the Old Bailey* Series 2 (Loftus Audio for BBC Radio 4).

Concerts/Other include: performer for The RADA Cabaret Company (2011–14), also conceiving, writing and directing shows; poetry recording and live performance for Live Canon Ensemble, including Winchester's Live Advent Calendar 2015, and Burns Nights for Oxford Playhouse and Greenwich Theatre; Period dance performer with Nonsuch History & Dance.

About Park Theatre

Park Theatre was founded by Artistic Director, Jez Bond. The building opened in May 2013 and, with three West End transfers, two National Theatre transfers and ten national tours in its first four years, quickly garnered a reputation as a key player in the London theatrical scene. In 2015 Park Theatre received an Olivier nomination and won The Stage's Fringe Theatre of the Year.

Park Theatre is an inviting and accessible venue, delivering work of exceptional calibre in the heart of Finsbury Park. We work with writers, directors and designers of the highest quality to present compelling, exciting and beautifully told stories across our two intimate spaces.

Our programme encompasses a broad range of work from classics to revivals with a healthy dose of new writing, producing in-house as well as working in partnership with emerging and established producers. We strive to play our part within the UK's theatre ecology by offering mentoring, support and opportunities to artists and producers within a professional theatre-making environment.

Our Creative Learning strategy seeks to widen the number and range of people who participate in theatre, and provides opportunities for those with little or no prior contact with the arts.

In everything we do we aim to be warm and inclusive; a safe, welcoming and wonderful space in which to work, create and visit.

★★★★★ 'A five-star neighbourhood theatre.' *Independent*

As a registered charity [number 1137223] with no public subsidy, we rely on the kind support of our donors and volunteers. To find out how you can get involved visit **parktheatre.co.uk**

Staff List

FISHSKIN TROUSERS

Elizabeth Kuti

For Jess, Robert, Brett and Eva

'El teatro es la poesía que se levanta del libro
y se hace humana…'

Lorca

'Orford Ness is emblematic of not only the Cold War, but also of the whole of twentieth-century warfare. During this period the systematic application of scientific principles to the development of weapons and warfare resulted in the ability of one country to subject an opponent to the threat of 'total war' across oceans or continents. This came to be known as MAD – Mutually Assured Destruction... The legacy of the site's recent military past also presents many hazards... it will always be a hostile and potentially dangerous place.'

National Trust Guide to Orford Ness, 2003

'Are all feral children autistic? From what we have just discussed it may be inferred that an unduly high proportion of feral children suffered from autism before they were abandoned. Indeed autism with its often severe conduct problems may be the cause for the abandonment in the first place. On the other hand, it would be ridiculous to assume that all feral children would be autistic. There are, no doubt, different reasons for young children being lost, hidden, isolated or abandoned, and different reasons for their survival in isolation.'

Uta Frith, Autism, *1987*

The Wild Man of Orford

From the Chronicles of Ralph of Coggeshall, Essex (1187)

In the time of King Henry II, when Bartholomew de Glanville was castellan of the castle of Orford, it happened that some fishermen who were fishing in the sea caught a wild man in their nets. At this, the castellan of Orford was lost in wonder. The wild man was completely naked and all his limbs were formed like those of a man. He was hairy and his beard was long and pointed. Around the chest he was very rough and shaggy. The castellan placed him under guard, day and night, and would not allow him to return to the sea. He eagerly ate anything that was brought to him. He devoured fish raw rather than cooked, squeezing the raw fishes in his hands until all of the moisture was removed and then eating them. He did not wish to talk, or rather did not have the power to talk, even when suspended by his feet and tortured. On being led into the church, he showed no sign of belief or of reverence and he did not genuflect or bow his head when he saw anything holy. He always sought out his bed at sunset and always lay there until sunrise.

[Eventually] it happened that they led the wild man back to the harbour. They placed three lines of very strong nets all around him and then allowed him back into the sea. But quickly he sought the open water and dived under the nets, emerging on the other side out of the depths of the sea as spectators on the seashore looked on. Often he dived down and after a short time re-emerged again, as if he were mocking the onlookers because he had evaded their nets. After he had played for a while in the sea, and after all hope of recovering him was lost, he came back to the shore again of his own accord, and remained with them for two months. But after a short time, because of the negligence of those who were guarding him, the wild man secretly fled back to the sea and was never seen again.

Whether this was some sort of mortal man, or whether it was an evil spirit inside the body of a drowned man or whether it was some fish in human form, it is not easy to tell…

Characters

MAB, *in her late twenties; servant at Orford Castle, twelfth century*

BEN, *in his late twenties; radar scientist at Stanford, 1973*

MOG, *turning thirty; a teacher, 2003*

MAB

I knew the first minute there was to be some heavy business
between us

– from that very first minute I sin 'im – strung up by his feet
and howling – oh I certainly knew we had business all right –

And knew also that this time

There'd be no doubt

We would see it through –

To whatever end – or final chapter – had to be.

For that deep stir in my gut – this ache I got, this throb, in my
wound here – (*Touches the side of her head.*) the place I know
you from –

it were that that told me our business needed finishing this time;
no more sliding, no more look-away

But the end of it, when it came, was, I'll confess – unexpected –

Not that I'm a fearful girl

Run a mile jump a stile eat a country pancake?

Me and the girls by the stream

What about you, Mab Green?

Die by fire or die by drowning?

I'd take the sweet soft drown any day – so I'd always said – and
when it come to it – when I were thrown from the quay –

Do it proper, Mab. Me mam ud say. Don't get it all crossways,
start from the beginning.

So

It start the day the fishermen brung him in, the merman.

They catched 'im, see, out beyond the Ness. 'E come up in the haul. That were the story.

The boat were a good deep ways out, so it goos, the nets easy, and the fishermen dawsey from the early start… when on a sudden there's a great pull and the nets start sliding out and the boys are fightin to hold 'em – and in the great struggle, what do they see but this great man-fish, white flash of thigh and shoulder, great clumps of drenched hair flowin like seaweed – all over – wild – like a beast, they say –

'E near capsized 'em, and their amazement, of course, boundless.

A fish in the shape of a man, cry Manny Jolt, and the others, soft noodles, hollerin too – must have been a boat full of holler, with the three fishermen, Manny Jolt, Peter Hankin, and Little Ben the boat-boy, frightened for their silly skins, and the poor sea creature howling in the net, thrashin and thrashin to be free…

God and all his holy saints, breathe Little Ben, what in the name of Jesus have we brung up?

Peter Hankin is jabbering they'd better fling it deep agin – A monster from the deep, he bawl – can only mean hexes and witchery and all darkness and damage imaginable.

But Manny Jolt beg to differ, and Manny says, says 'e, let's tek him to the castellan – de Glanville, that is – Bartholomew de Glanville, he of the castle at Orford – de Glanville will reward them for a wonder such as this –

So – they brung the Wild Man in – and of course de Glanville, so I hear, can't believe his luck. Be that fish or merman, or dead sailor possessed by dark sea spirit or what all he be, de Glanville mean to be the revealer of the horrid story. Beside 'imself with glee no doubt with this miracle to be snouting inter.

Stupid bugger de Glanville, never liked him, the rutting dog, always pressing girls in corners filthy animal the ones too weak to stop him.

Well – there's mardle and bustle, and great whisper goin round the Castle that the fishermen hev net a monster, some wild man, or fish-man – they dunno… and Minnie Hinday's agitatin about the place – *they got that demon in the dark room below the basement – roped like a pig for the slaughter!* So what, Minnie Hinday, I say? Her eyes go huge and starin – *God, Mab*, she cry, *what kinda fool are you! Master's lorst is mind, 'e gorn and let the Devil in!*

Soppy daft gal that Minnie Hinday. I says as much to her.

But I'll confess I were curious. Same as everybody.

So when the men below want water an all to scrub that clean, I offers to go down with the pail and brushes, thinkin, well, be worth the toil down the stairs to see such a wonder

Well I git to the trapdoor in the basement – and it bolted down fast so I knock –

And I hear such strange cries and noises goin on below – *wah-wah-wah* and yowling and howling mixed with laughter –

And then this pitiful mew, high-pitched –

She mews high-pitched, an unearthly sound.

And grunts, and long shaking groans – like an animal that's caught and can't die – and I'm afeared and wonderin should I ditch the pail, run back up the stairs and look away from whatever's happening in the dark basement below but then the bolt clank back and I climb down into the dark prison chamber –

And what I see –

The Wild Man

Wrongways

Head down and that's feet high up roped near the ceiling and that's poor bloodshot eyes rolling and that's arms and neck chafing from the ropes

And all those sounds come from the Wild Man, with that's bulging throat, and mouth like a torn pocket –

And the blood trickle slowly

I dumps the pail and brushes and they set to, the boat-boys – they scrub at his shiny skin more naked and pitiful than a chicken plucked for cooking.

I got out then, didn't want to see no more.

Over the days though, I learned bits about you piecemeal, I strained my ears for tidings. De Glanville every day's inventing some new test to measure you by.

They brung you to church to see if you have any kind of soul. But you won't kneel in church nor bless yourself but howl and yabber like a babe at a christening full of demon.

No sound from you but jabber-jabber-wawl-wawl and sometimes that mewing when you're frightened and the flap-flap-flap when troubled.

They want you to speak but you won't.

Can't, I reckon to meself, but they think different.

They think he can but will not. They think he taunt them. He defy them. So they got him pig-wise, by the feet, and they drench him with icy water and they burn 'im, and they –

I sin the tongs, I sin the cleaver, I –

Defy? Taunt?

Who taunt who?

Was my question.

What they can't grasp –

If a creature can't speak –

He come from the sea, what can he speak, sea-words? Got a lungful of water, how can he breathe out what they want?

Whatsomiver they want anyhow?

What can he tell them?

How many toes on a mermaid? The smell of a conch? How many sides has a pearl?

Squit!

And then of course there's food. What to give the beast?

They're powerful fond of bugs beam Cook, but course 'e won't
take the rainy bugs and worms they gonned him. I knew he
would not, I said as much to Cook! So Cook say, you so clever,
Mab, what'll he take for victuals then? Red face sweatin at me.
Mab, hey, go on then, tell us, if you be so wise in the ways of
the fish-folk!

Says I, I dunno, Cook – a bit cautious-like cos there's a rum
edge to her sneer and I don't like it – I dunno nothing about no
fish-folk, be dashed if I dew, I say.

Can't even hazard a guess, Mab? We all heard about you and
your secret dips – Like a sea-witch, ent you, Mab Green, love to
be waved-on, she do, out in the splash when it get choppy – and
all wise and Christian folk are home by the fire!

Mebbe that's why you ent got no husband and you close to thirty!

Cook got little flecks of summat nasty at the corner of her
mouth, dried spittle, bit of spit-froth, like some venomous bite
she just waiting to discharge.

I look at her cool-like though inside my heart goo bang-bang
bang-bang like I'll bust.

Fish, I say. I wager the thing'll eat fish.

Cook near reel orf her fat feet.

What fried, baked, what?

Raw, I say, in a bucket. I'll give it him.

So I do.

Nice big bucket of pretty shiny fish, all gleaming eyes and
glinting coats

Wild Man devour with joy the little creatures. He'd delve in the
bucket and pull one out, croon over it and smell it, and always
before he put it in his mouth – for I watched him close, delighted
by his pleasure in the food – he went through a strange little
dancing ritual of touching it, the fish, to nose, to cheek, to lips,
first left, then right, then up, then down, then back and forth
again, three or four times – and then at last – in! He'd cram it in
and chew with fierce concentration spitting out the bones before
shaping and brushing them into a neat little pile.

I did it every night. It became my task, to take the fish to him before sunset.

For the moment sunset came he always went instantly to bed. Lying motionless, eyes open. I never saw him sleep, but they say he never moved an inch till dawn.

So fetching and so dear his tidy ways.

I feeds 'im and I watch 'im eat. And so goo the days.

Until all of a sudden – the day come when I sin what I seen – and then I knows – and everythin changes –

BEN

BEN, *twenty-eight, tie, shirt, glasses.*

So, it's January, 1973, and I'm stuck on this crazy English island, Orford Ness – and I'm making long-distance calls to my mum in Australia – Canberra – Woden Valley, to be precise – trying to distract her from the fact that I'm twenty-eight and don't have a girlfriend.

Okay, so get this, Mum, I was telling her – they've got this new theory about time, Mum, this idea that time is not so much like a line – starting back in the past and going on forward into the future – but more, if you can picture this, okay, more like a *balloon*, right, imagine a balloon being blown up… so it starts out kind of small and wrinkled but then gradually it gets bigger and bigger –

And then imagine there's some stuff drawn or written on the balloon, say like, a little picture or whatever, and as the balloon blows up this picture gets bigger too, but also there's more room for other pictures on the balloon, cos it's a bigger and bigger balloon, right…

And that's like time –

It expands, and there's more and more of it… but – and here's the crucial thing, Mum – as time expands, *everything that ever was there, is there still!*

Nothing gets erased!

Everything remains on the balloon and it just gets bigger and bigger and bigger...

Till what? she says   We all go pop?

Actually you're right, Mum, we go pop, and the balloon collapses and turns into a black hole.

A black hole? Great – a new reason to be depressed... and what are you doing out there in England anyway?

Sorry, Mum, it's kind of classified – gotta go!

Okay, so the story in Orford Ness was that they had some kind of issue with the fancy new Over the Horizon radar system they'd installed

Bloody Poms! Typical.

It's supposed to be an A-one fail-safe system can monitor Warsaw Pact aircraft, with a key focus on the Northern Missile Test Centre at Plesetsk... except there is some kind of – low-level interference, ground clutter, environmental I'd say... Basically, in layman's terms, the readings from the radar – codename Cobra Mist, that's what they call it, the radar – well, the readings were indecipherable because of this weird noise getting in the way.

So the UK military get on to my boss at Stanford, Professor Lindstrom, and we're all flown out here to fix it.

They've put me on the island – the Ness – and all day I'm taking the readings –

'Three oh four seven slash two nine eight point four seven nine lateral beam maximum variation thirty-seven to the thirty-ninth – '

The console's in this basement cell, with no windows, and neon strip lighting in your eyes all day and no proper ventilation – what a shit-hole...

So, by the time they have us ferried back across to Orford town every night at six p.m., I'm in serious need of liquid refreshment.

I'll say one thing for Suffolk – there's another asset in addition to cowshit and buttercups and that is ye olde traditional English pub and their crazy beer. Bishop's Finger!

The girl behind the bar at The Jolly Sailor has a nice arse and Christ now I'm on the subject the front view's... not so dusty either.

Some kind of Irish name – what was it? Moira? Monica?

Cute girl.

What was it? Mabel?

Mabel...

I'm just waiting to make my killer move.

Mabel doesn't know this yet, but I'm actually a big success story. Back home, especially. They had my picture in the *Woden Valley Advertiser* a few years back. I was big news in the suburbs – not just a scholarship to the States but *Stanford*. Mum just couldn't get her face right.

I'd always done okay – well, more than okay, at university, and my Prof recommended radar science, said it was an up-and-coming area given the current political climate et cetera. So I did my masters, and then it turns out my thesis is this big success and it even got published –

And then suddenly it seems like everyone – I mean everyone – is offering me scholarships for my PhD – not just at home but in the States as well – So I pick Stanford, Californ-I-A.

That's when I started working with Professor Lindstrom – who is kind of a creep but also a radar genius – and Stanford is great.

It's great.

No worries.

I fit in. From the minute I arrived. Made sure of that.

I get my PhD under my belt in record time, and then the Prof takes me on as a post-doc, gets me this fellowship, full-time, and we're working on this radar research project and hey, the funding is unbelievable, and the expenses, and the international conferences... and despite my mother's lectures about grandchildren and what about that lovely Ruth around the corner who I used to play tennis with... I'm hanging out on the beach in LA with Mandie and Sandie and Candie and all my new buddies and...

I've never claimed to be perfect. And I should have stuck up for Mikey, but who could have known – none of us could have known –

I should have spoken. And I didn't. There's a lot of fear on campus, it gets to you, you do things – people do things, the crowd thing, it gets out of control –

Of course the downside of time being a balloon, and everything that has ever happened is happening still is that –

Well if it's all still happening –

All the things you ever did –

you can think of some things you'd like to consign – really consign – to the dustbin of history shall we say –

Dr Cooper – he's the campus psychiatrist – I told him the whole story – how Mike died – and he kept saying five years was long enough and I should try to see the verdict of the inquest as closure – a line drawn under what happened.

He said everybody makes mistakes. It's not so easy being a foreigner.

And I really shouldn't let one unhappy incident obstruct my academic career.

So – I've been doing fine, the last couple of years.

But when Lindstrom suddenly gets this urgent call from London, and he's looking for a research team to come to the UK – and what with one thing and another – I kind of feel like a break from campus life would be maybe a good idea. Put some distance –

So I put my hand up. And Lindstrom picked me. *Voilà*.

And here we are.

It's going fine – I'm on the console – nights at The Jolly Sailor –

Just every so often I kept getting this really terrible –

Some kind of anomaly.

This terrible noise.

A high-pitched intense piercing sound – it was like –

It kind of reminded me of –

It was driving me crazy if you want to know.

So I decided to check it out – Took some equipment and went walkabout round the island taking readings. Until I saw a pattern.

It was when I got out towards the shoreline, beyond the lighthouse, that the readings intensified.

In fact – when I took my shoes off and waded out into the water – the readings began to go mad – it was like I was getting close to what seemed to be the source – the epicentre, of this weird noise –

blasting my freaking ears off through the head-phones

I said to Lindstrom – what do you make of that? Some kind of electronic signal coming from below the water?

Like from a sub or something? Why would it be spiking in this very localised position? Could this even be what we're looking for – the anomaly? Is it auroral disturbance? The noise clutter that's screwing up the radar?

Anomaly? Lindstrom says, I don't know what you're talking about, Ben, we got ground scatter, we're not looking for auroral disturbance.

Yeah but, Prof, I took the readings, I said… Yesterday. They were all there on my screen.

But Lindstrom's gone, off to beat the Russkies.

I got the readings though, just off the shingle beach beyond Lantern Marsh. This anomaly – it was all there on the graphs. High-pitched, high-frequency, intense noise.

Like a scream.

MOG

So I'd had this week, the week from hell, and I was doing eighty
Down the motorway, just driving, thinking – where am I going?
How the hell did I get here? When did this end begin?
Where did it start? To go so horribly off-track?
The Aurora Borealis.
Was that it?

Daniel went to Norway, saw the Northern Lights.
The Aurora Borealis. He did an assembly about it.
I can't remember really, quite the point –
Apart from look at me with my bloody lovely holidays.
Oh yeah – the Gifts of Nature. The Environment.
Aurora Borealis. I wonder what Wendy thought.
I wonder if –
He phoned me, Daniel. From a Norwegian phonebox
He'd found on one of his 'evening walks'.
What's that? The evening-adultery walk?
Wendy wasn't wise to that one yet.
Dan said don't text or email, so I didn't.
Norwegian phoneboxes seem to work fantastically well.
I heard him crystal-clear, after the time delay
Like when you throw a penny down a cool deep well
And wait to hear the splash. I understand. I understand.
Yes of course you must. Not endanger your marriage
I get that, we never should have – it's fine, it's fine –
I let him go. Like a penny down a well.

Plink.

Gone.

So now we're on this environmental kick

Big project, save the Earth, whole-school effort

We're collecting – bottle tops, cartons, disused mobiles

Plastic bags, organic waste, chicken shit

I told Year Five about this birthday approaching

This major birthday that I wasn't so crazy about

Three whole decades and it's quite a landmark

Quite a moment of shall we say reflection.

I told them I'd be celebrating this weekend

So deeply that I might not make it back for Monday.

Little Grace came in next day; something in her pocket.

What is it, Grace? Not her name. She gave up on telling us

How to say her name and asked for Grace instead;

We gratefully agreed. 'For you, Miss Green.' A box, she gave me

Wrapped in tissue paper with a bow on top.

How exciting! – popping it away, for later,

Much more touched than I can let them see –

And thank you so very very much.

It's recycled. A gift of nature. I made it for your birthday, miss.

Did you, Grace? I can hardly wait! And now, the register –
    Tanisha?

I said I hoped to make it back for Monday ha ha ha.

And if I didn't – if for some reason – I partied
So hard that I fell off a cliff and couldn't make it back –
They were to continue with the project –
And there'd be a really nice replacement cover teacher
An awful lot nicer and more funny than me
With much nicer shoes. I promise. I promise.
Their faces looked a bit confused so I hastened I was joking
I'll be back on Monday!
I guess – we'll see –
We'll see

Thing is
What they told me – at the hospital –
It really frightened me, I can't pretend it didn't
Cos it did and I don't scare easy no I don't
But they – they have all these machines –
They looked at you, you see, so safe inside
Curled up inside, my little dot, my little remnant –
And let's be honest I don't give a fuck about Dan
Dan's got what's his and he's sticking with it as he should
And you are what is left – and you are mine –
You are mine, in me, from me, and I will have you.
So I thought. No question.

Okay so what happened then is, they smeared on this jelly
And they do this weird thing with a – they make a picture
Out of sound, the noise you make, your pretty somersaults,

And they convert the blips into a picture, on a screen
A noise picture – your first ever kind of photo and it
Sounds kind of sweet till she used the word anomaly.

Not too cold that jelly for you? The scan-lady says squinting
No. Lovely. Let's have a look then.

And there's you on this screen, I see you, I spy –
Moving, turning, transforming, becoming –
And the word *darling* rises up in me so sweet.
It's like all the passion, shall we call it, was not erased
But made this nuclear explosion that was you

I'm on the plastic-couch thing but floating quite enchanted
As she sweeps her little squeezy radar back and forth –
And then –

I wait for it to end but it – goes on; there's this – shift –
The quiet's gone utter, thick and still; she sweeps again
And I ask – but she stops me with a 'just one moment' –
White coat zips off behind a screen and there's a murmured call
And by and by another white coat and they are searching
What? What? I want to shout but years of good behaviour
Strangles me, throat clenches tight – Is anything…? –
I'm trying to sound normal – bat it away
This dark sense of terrible news and when it comes
It is so terrible that I'm dry as death and tears don't come –

She offers Kleenex
Pointlessly.

We think — we can't be sure – there may be an –
Anomaly – some kind of problem, the lower-left leg
We're not seeing
The typical bone development we'd expect
We're not quite sure – we'll look again – new appointment –
The machine trundles on. Appointments.
Consultants. The kind, the not-so-kind, the daily grind
Of life and death, mundane, apocalyptic, all in one.
The prognosis emerges after some deliberating –
The impact of the problem they've detected
The lower-left leg
But – prosthetics now – so much improved –
Yes, deformity – anomaly – but advances all the time –
Though we know – that's hard to – deal with – disability –
It's hard to process and we'd understand if on balance –
They don't say it but those words are there – *on your own*
Lone mother
We would be able to arrange a –
We do see from your history –
A certain tendency towards –
It's all here on your notes –
Going back some years –
Prozac – Temazepam –
We'd sign the forms –

You do have options –
If you felt you needed
To discontinue.

Which is funny really.
Because –

I said, I've thought a lot quite lately –
And in the past!
Of *discontinuing* –
Thought of it a lot
Over the years
Don't you see
I'd love to scream
This isn't random
I'm being punished
God just hates me
And then it all blurts out
The way I just don't get *happy*
Like other people get it –
It's over there, I know
I just don't feel it.
I get these black-dog thoughts,
I always have
Dan used to say I needed help,
I said I needed

Other stuff.

And I thought for once –

I thought – *but I've got you now*

So when they said you'd

Come out wrong,

A life of struggle

People staring

And *all my fault* –

So I caved in; said I couldn't cope; they signed the forms

Gave me the pills and the instructions.

The pills they use to terminate –

The unviable, unwanted, hopeless –

Mistakes of nature, mistakes –

They seemed to want me to –

And I want to – not cause trouble –

Or what it is I want – I really don't know

I want –

The pills they have to cut you loose.

You take two in the evening; two next morning.

Then go in to the hospital with an overnight bag.

Twenty-four hours and it – you – should all be over.

So that was my week, the week from hell, and the reason why

I was flooring it down the motorway going nowhere – until! –

Flash of revelation! I realise that where I want to go – is *home* –

Then wondering what that means? When – da da! I see the
    junction!

The old familiar number beckons like the star to Bethlehem –

I swerve and –

Orford. The Castle. My old house. Jolly Sailor, St Bartholemews

How quaint.

We upped sticks and scarpered years ago, soon as my mum
    Mabel

Had stashed away her barmaid's wages, got enough

For art school and a flat in Peckham, the dream she chased –

Just me and Mum, Mabel and me. I never met my dad. He died.

But somehow, Orford, I don't know –

It smells like home.

There's no people left I know, the old are dead, the young
    deserted.

Some friends I recognise: there's rosemary, abundant

By the church gate; gulls scream and words still linger

Reminding me of stuff I lost – the mermaid's purse

I found aged nine and kept beside my bed; the muntjac's skull.

They flood back in, the words, all out of season, jumbled:

Sea-campion, thrift and samphire;

Rainy bugs and gorse;

And the Ness, the island, those distant pagodas

Where they dabbled with the atom; spied on the Reds.

There's lots of fear round here.

So there I am, back home, pitched up off season; a B and D is
    easy.

Dump bags and – oh, the gift from Grace –

The little box in tissue paper – I'll unwrap it

On my birthday, as I promised, so I take it

And off we go – ready for the weekend!

The four white pills are in my rucksack. It's decided.

I tell myself, I'll need some water. So I get some in a bottle.

Then – Do I say goodbye?

What do I say?

A phrase swims in my thoughts *Christ have mercy*

Think – *where did that come from?* even as it comes again

Lord have mercy Christ have mercy Lord have mercy

Those ancient words I didn't know I knew

MAB

Why I didn't think before – I dunno!

Fool Mab!

Took me so long to see it!

Ringin in me, pealin away like a bell won't bloody stop –

For I sin 'em do it –

Mam and Fa – they did what they did

I sin 'em, I were there, and all I saw, and I ent never ever tol no
one because –

Cos I knew what they did was bad beyond all daily badness

And what they did, it killed Fa – stone dead, oh that I knew, it
drove 'im to – what 'e did – the rope – the beam –

Stop, Mab, stop and take it piece by piece.

So. What happened, gal, says you?

I brung the merrow down the fish bucket as always, supper
time, and I sees 'im squeeze 'em dry in's fists and gulp 'em as
'e always do.

They got 'im roped as usual, round his ankles to the rings in the
wall, which is why ol' Manny is nodding off, I see that all right,
Manny snoring, strong fume of ale about the place, he'll not
wake I'd say.

And it's then I sees his foot flex up and spread itself like a fan,
or fin, it come up and spread out, so I can see between each toe
a web of skin, taut as a drum –

so delicate the light can pass straight through till it gleam quite
golden –

Two feet 'e got webbed like some magical goose, like some
swan child or leaping frog – like – like – like what?

And I grope and reach for it and this time up it swim right up
out of the seafloor of my unremembered life –

That other golden web-footed creature come back to me –
Mab's playfellow, Mab's other half –

How we race out along the sand and you never so happy as you
could be when being waved on, my dear little sprout, you was
severed from me, and I got the wound to prove it, here by the side
of my head, where our flesh fused, where you and me was one –

the handywoman did deliver us she screamed and got her knife
and quick as sin my mother said, rived us apart, right through
the join that had fused us my ear to your stomach –

leavin us bloody both but both still bawling, breathing,

And we grew and prospered, never parted, as though her knife
could cut the skin but not the soul

And you was such a strange little morsel of God's love, with
your *wah-wah-wah* and your *mog-og-og-og* so Mog, we called
you, my Mog, my other half. And oh such a strange bewitching
creature, so restive like an April day, but plain you moved with
all things natural and good, roared only when life got too wordy
or too loudy

And you raced through the water like a seal, gleaming a trail of
boyflesh through the waves, and I go too because I'm a watery
one as well

But Mam and Fa they think it's witchy, that it bode them ill,
they don't understand your flap-flap-flap and no-word world,
your non-compliance – thass all they got, foolish angry words,
don't mean squit, exist in air and vanish. But they are troubled
so, they think you prove they failed or sinned, and that no
man'll touch me cos of you.

An I see all that – it leap up in my heart – and drenched I am by
this flood of long-ago –

That day – aged what? Five, or mebbe six? – could not be more
– when they took us two a trip, rowed out to the Ness. Fa row
the long way out – all the way round to the other side, the
shingle beach out beyond Lantern Marsh. Fa ties up to a
mooring post, and we run off and play, while Mam do what she
has to, some boring task, gather stones, she says. For what? I
think but then care less.

All day we're there, till dusk is fallin, then I hear 'em call –

Time for tea? I ask – they nod. Mam she turn to the side, and I
see a great spew of vomit torrent from her mouth and splash out
upon the shingle –

Mam's sick I think, oh dear, we must get home – and we pulls
out the boat, climbs in, and I'm drowsy from the sun, layin
gentle in the boat, but with half-closed eyes I see that Mam is
fussin at you with some strange thing, some little waistcoat that
she's made you. Put this on, she says, and you go flap-flap-flap
and mew, don't like it, but she jams it on, each sleeve, and it
looks wrong, all bulgey, pockets stuffed with –

Hey I shout, why's he got one, not me? Not fair!

I'm cold! I whine… and you're screeching, screeching, gurgling, miserable, and when I reach out towards you my hand knocks against the new waistcoat's hard-and-heavy bulging pockets, full of – what? Coins? I think, and shout – Why's he get coins not me? I'm the one can use 'em! Not that simpleton, I scream! What's money to a fool?

Them were the words.

Mab, you shut it, hiss my father, and bash me so I'm sprawling face-down in the bottom of the boat, and now they've flung something a top of me, a bunch of net, it stinks, I'm caught, and in the dark, and in the net, I hear nothing, but the flap-flap jabber of you jerkin like a landed fish in that strange heavy waistcoat

a grunt comes out of Mam and she spew some more and Fa does nothing

Till of a sudden he stoop down and scoop you up into his arms so small a bundle but then I see him take a strange spinnin turn like a dance almost and then I see him hurl out with all his might just one grunting howl as his arms open wide release and let you fly –

Away over the side of the boat

And the scream in that moment – whose – it's Mam's, it's mine, or Fa

Or yours, or all of us

this scream I hear, goos on and on, piercin, screamin

And the moment of you flyin out it last and last it never end

Lord have mercy Christ have mercy Lord have mercy Christ have mercy

The scream –

Whose throat I dunno

That scream goo on long after – can't make it stop

Hear it always

scream down the years

screamin the decades

pierce every corner of the sky, in my skull

Won't stop

Never

Boat bob, I must be out like a candle.

When I come to, Mam and Fa have pulled in, moored up, and lugged me out –

We're at the quay. Deserted. Hardly any moon.

No one sin us though we creep like thieves in any case

Stumble home, put one foot before the other.

The house is dark, we crawl inside. Mam, Fa and me.

I lays down. I think – *not coins. But stones. Sewn in the pockets.*

Bed swoop and shudder

Turn to the wall me.

We none of us

Years goo by

say nothing.

All this

All of it

The scream

Come back

In less than a heartbeat as I see his curious fins fan out

My hand's still grasped around the ankle of the merman

And I stare and stare at the great lithe twist of him

From his foot to his knee and thigh, groin and haunch

To chest and shoulder, neck, back and arms

And sweeping down am drawn at last to that strange grazed

Shape upon his stomach, not seen till now, sealed-up scar

So salmon pink against his flesh – relic of a wound.

The wound that matches mine!

BEN

So I'm back at The Jolly Sailor that night, thinking, I saw it on
the screen, right, a high-frequency noise or signal, just off the
shingle beach – why would Lindstrom block me? Does it not fit
his results? Is this stuff classified?

Or am I just insane?

And I'm troubled by all this work shit but then – the beer kicks
in and I'm noting Mabel's mellifluous form behind the bar... I
stroll up and order a Scotch and Mabel says she's on a break
now and when I say oh really care to join me for a drink
expecting a frosty English elbow she says in such a really quite
endearing English way yes that would be lovely.

So I get her a midi – they love their beer these Suffolk babes –
and we settle by the fire, a little formal – age? Name?
Occupation? Respectively twenty-eight, Mabel Green, barmaid,
but would-be art-school student – she smiles – and time flies by.

Then: I guess I should be going. You really must? I say.

Well I mustn't keep you from your research, she says, saving us
from the Reds, I mean, it would be awful if you got distracted
and we all got nuked or something? Besides, my shift don't end
until eleven.

I'll come back then, I say, before I even think it. How about a little – walk? After your shift?

If you like, she says; that's good, I say, I'll see you then, eleven.

I meet her at the door outside, she's there with bag and coat and waiting when I come back, fresh shirt, but nothing too obvious, don't wanna look like I'm trying – though I am suddenly really trying – we walk and – do I flatter myself or is she nervous? – she witters on about some project – for her art portfolio – this concept she's exploring – clothes from fishskin – it's an experiment –

But suddenly – she stops, says –

Listen!

…

I can't hear anything, I say.

Don't you hear that? She says. Like a bell? Underwater?

I – I don't, I blurt, what do ya mean, I – ?

Like a bell tolling – like the bell tower's under the sea? There are whole towns here that the sea's taken, like where the cliffs collapsed at Dunwich and everything, houses, schools, church and bells, they're lying, somewhere, beneath the waves – some nights you hear it – there! listen! There!

No, I don't hear it. Sorry.

The moment's gone, she looks suddenly embarrassed – so I hurry to assure her –

That's weird, you know – I hear things too.

What kinds of things?

Stuff out on the island.

You mean, the stuff you're looking for? Russian submarines?

Well, yes, I guess, I mean that's what the radar's for, Cobra Mist –

What's Cobra Mist, she says, and in her mouth it's like a spell.

What they call it, their OTH system –

What's OTH?

Over the Horizon – that's their radar system – the readings are – well, unreadable. They're picking up this extra noise, ground clutter, they can't figure it out.

But – I've been hearing this other thing, this noise – like your bell – I dunno – it's kind of weird – it's registering on my screen, it was there today – but my boss – Professor Lindstrom – he's refusing to accept my results –

What kind of noise? She says.

Like a – I dunno – it's terrible – like a – well, the sound pattern is this – intense, piercing, high-pitched –

Scream? She says.

The signal's strongest on the beach out beyond Lantern Marsh – a little way out in the water. Lindstrom says I'm imagining it.

They always say that. And Mabel looks quite soft and sad.

No, but, Mabel – I'm not imagining it – cos the weirdest thing – it's only in this localised position – just offshore – at particular coordinates –

Why don't we go? says Mabel. Have a look.

Go where?

Out to the island, says Mabel. Let's go and listen.

What now? What – swim?

Row, says Mabel. I've got a boat. My uncle's. It's in the quay.

You do? You have a boat?

The tide'll be right for another two hours, says Mabel. We can always come back.

And I guess I'm so bewitched by her –

We take the boat and go –

MOG

So I'm on the quay at Orford all chips and whisky
And self-pity in my wet cagoule – when I see the boats!
And think, why not? We did it often – teenage kicks,
Nick a boat, row out to the Ness, light a fire, drink cider –
And the idea appeals to me more and more
Some kind of ceremony, some revisiting of misspent youth
Get pissed and do this pill thing and get out.
It is my birthday, after all.
So I grab a boat, and off we go, and it's
Not so dusty, rowing on the gentle lapping waves,
Out to the looming Ness. *Be careful, Mog,*
Mabel's voice, my mother, I hear her, same as always,
Don't you go there, Mog, keep away from the Ness
S'all right, Ma, I know your stories, fairies in the harebells
And Tom-Tit-Tot – whole towns beneath the waves – such
    squit –
Not squit she said, *spirit-logged, we are, these parts, the water*
Drags 'em in and holds 'em. And your father – Okay, Mabel
You hippy, even if you are just a voice in my head
Could we please put a sock in it? Not this story now.
Just saying, Mog, be careful of the Ness, the tides –
It's dangerous. You ent sin it. Your father's body
Washed up three weeks after he went missin in the sea
And that's a sight I never will forget. I roll my eyes –
And think, he should have been more careful, Ma!
I thought Australians knew about tides and sharks

And God knows what, isn't that their forte?

Couldn't he have tried to stay alive long enough at least

To meet me – once? Just once? Is that so much to ask?

Ma's voice again: *You're angry, Mog, but anger's*

Like a black dog.

I'm not angry, Ma, I say out loud, I'm rowing.

I'm rowing, me, in this little boat, I'm dealing

With it all!

Without you.

The Ness she welcomes me, white arms held out.

I step ashore – see cold moon, clear light –

And hear a sound – the distant pealing of a bell.

So this is it.

Here's where I cut you loose.

MAB

And soon as I know who you are – I think – that's it – this time
I got to save you –

and I hev my knife and I saw and I saw at the rope until –
you're free –

– and I pull you up and drag you, whispering hush now, we got
to get you out – push up the trapdoor with its iron bolts and
shove you through – but now there's stairs and stairs –

your feet and legs don't go so well on stone as in the water –

and if I'm caught they'll kill me, that I know – and you are
stumbling and near falling all the time, your hands flop and

your feet do little girlish steps on your tippy-toes like a baby
learning to walk and I catch at you but somehow you right
yourself and call *Wah wah wah wah* and *mog-og-og-og-og* to
the full bright moon – my Mog, we called you, for those funny
sounds! – and on we goo, get through the east gate to the street
and to the quay and quite by chance or by the action of the
angels, it seem no one's around, must be all at the fireplace,
eating stew, or doing what they do indoors –

And by the grace of God I find Fa's boat, and I near push you
in, not too bad a leap, because the tide is high, and I know that's
where I must take you – to the Ness, and the shingle shore
where Mam and Fa – that's where we'll go –

– and as I row, perhaps because I can't believe we've got away,
but I'm laughing and crowing with pure delight because – I had
it wrong! What I thought they did, they didn't do! They didn't
snuff you out – far from it – you must have swum away from
that murderous boat, out-swum the heavy waistcoat and grew
and thrived – became the goodly creature that you are today,
well-formed and beautiful in your own particular way –

And the Ness looms up, keeping its secrets, as it always has,
sucking its souls and spirits deep into its quiet centre – and I
drag the boat to shore – when on a sudden I feel your strong
arms round me and you pull me out to where the waves will
toss us and turn us as we used to love so dearly – and first the
freezing water make me scream – till suddenly the pain goes
and we are swimming as we used to, as we did as childer, out in
the splash, all choppy, and waved on –

But I am not your kind. I don't belong. And I know I have to
leave you here, or they'll follow us and catch you. So I wade to
the boat –

But he won't let go, my Mog, he mewing, hand clawing at my
back, and tapping at my hid, and his dear face so close that I
can't see him except his eyes …

Go back now Mog, I whisper, our faces close together. Let go.

My boat bobs out, the tide is pullin me away – and I leave you
there again – It rip me like it did the first time when they rived
us – but I grit my teeth and row and row –

BEN

Mabel, it turns out, is not only cute but one hell of an
oarswoman –

She brings us round to the eastern shore; we moor up, and then
crunch for a while along the shingle beach, then sit, and huddle
close beneath my coat. She has a spliff – we share it – and she
says God this must be boring after California and I say actually
I'm from Woden Valley, a little-known suburb of Canberra...
which brings whole new levels to the concept of boring. And
she laughs and says *Woden*, that's so *weird* – and I say hey,
Mabel, did you know time's like a balloon and we are giggling
like mad people and – it's all going really well –

And she's like – Ben, Ben, do you wanna see my art project I
was tellin you about?

Gallant as Sir Galahad, I go – You betcha –

So she pulls out these – things from her bag, these crazy
trousers, and yes, they're actually made of fishskins! They glint,
in the moonlight – rainbows coming off them – And I'm like –
Far out! Mabel, you are avant-garde! It's like a like a silver zoot
suit, man – You could flog these to a rock star – David Bowie!

She says, *Squit!* Then giggles. *You put 'em on! Ben, go on! Put
'em on!*

What, get undressed?

Go on, she says. Get your keks off, mate!

So I do!

And I'm kind of dancing around in the fishskin trousers and
they feel good, I'm feelin good, and it's all sort of pretty funny
till she says, God Ben, you look amazing...

Which I take as my cue. To get serious. And I kiss her and –
well, a whole lot more, I won't bore you with the details but
suffice to say – the cold doesn't really seem to be a problem for
quite a while...

And when we've finished –

we're lying on the shingle, hardly got our breath back yet, and it's January, for Chrissakes, so I get the coat to cover us again – and she coughs and says look I don't usually do this –

Then she's staring straight at me. Strangely.

What?

Why are you crying? She says.

And fuck me it's true, when I touch my face, the tears are pouring down my cheeks

And suddenly – I – I'm seeing Mike, Mike Tomiyoshi – my roommate – five years ago, the night he died – it's just all there, coming back, in technicolour –

And I try to fight it, avoid the triggers, like Cooper showed me, but I can't, it's rising out of me, like vomit –

and I don't know why, but for the first time I want to tell it – I want to tell the whole story – to her – and it all comes out – how I came back to my fraternity late that night and I heard this screaming and – when I opened the door to the basement, some of the guys were there, and they had Mike strung up by the feet in his underpants and they were dowsing him with water and slapping him and I was like, what the hell? And they said Sigma Alpha tradition, Ben: this is the consummation, we need to be tougher on the pledges this year and Mike was kind of puking and whimpering. So I said, hey fellas, come on, now, cut him down, looks like he's had enough, and they said – oh he's had enough alright, we helped him drink five gallons – perhaps you'd like to try it? Course if we'd known the little Gook was your friend – like they thought they were in Vietnam or something –

And I laughed and I said, me, me? I'm Aussie, mate; we hate the fucking Gooks as much as anybody!

Those were the words.

I walked away from the basement, went back to my room, to my desk and began jotting down formulae.

They cut Mike down then and put him in the boot of a car and drove off to a lake, and I don't know what happened but next

day this woman walking her dog found him and he was dead.
So the college authorities investigated as did the police and the
verdict of the inquest was that it was an accident. Excess of
high spirits. There was swelling of the brain from all the water.
A joke that went too far.

When I read back the formulae I'd written in my book, they
were unreadable, my hand must have been shaking so much.

Mabel listens, till I finish. Then she draws away – staring out
towards the waves – shivering – and her fingers are sort of
flapping or drumming, on the shingle, and I want her to speak
but she says nothing – just flap-flap-flap – what the hell is
wrong with you, I begin to think, shivering too, say something
for Chrissake, if you hate me, just tell me!

And then –

Hear that? she says.

and I do – it's high-pitched – strange – yowling – like a –

Do you hear a bell? she breathes.

I wish I did, but what I hear's high-pitched – like a – more like
a scream – building and building in intensity – coming from just
offshore – a little ways out into the water –

And Mabel starts grabbing at me, pulling at me – the bell
beneath the waves, you hear it, Ben? The bell?

There's no goddamn bell, Mabel, what are you nuts? I scream,
trying to get this crazy witch-girl off me – There's no bell here –
you must be fucking crazy – there's a terrible – howling – do
you not hear it – like a scream –

And I push her off me and run like fuck into the wind, into the
darkness, still in the fishskin trousers, this knife in my head,
the wind –

Ben!

And the noise I'm hearing – it can't be anything but that auroral
disturbance I was getting and I think if maybe I go right into it –
shut that fucking scream up, shut the fucker up –

MOG

I cross the island and make towards the sea, like it draws me

I'm on the eastern side in a hollow dip of coastline,

And the waves are lapping

And my hand closes on the packet of pills – now or never –

The bell – what bell? – it's tolling and it's midnight; fuck, my
  birthday!

Thirty years good Christ and what to show –

A whole new decade looming – and all those candles

Standing up on cakes, armies of them, all extinguished,

Yet here I am, alone. Where are my people?

I bellow to the futile skies and pointless waves

And empty stars and vacant heavens –

And think of you – my little dot –

And what I'm about to do – and I'm another

Useless mother, but better you should know it now

Than live to learn it later! Mothers suck. They're shoving you
  away

From the minute that they push you out – sad truth!

Welcome to the world!

I hear a scream – kids? Cats? Fornicating?

Or someone on the Ness like me – here to commit

A murder?

As if to brace myself I stand and face the sea

Take out two pills, see them on my hand

And raise them to my lips, when – wham! my balance

Falters, I stumble on some driftwood – my hand jerks out,

The pills fly off, white flash, then gone for ever,
Lost for ever in the shingle, impossible to find
I know, no point even trying, and raging, cursing –
Sobbing with the shock, I roar in pain –
Can't even do that right! Black dogs gnaw at me,
Growling, snarling, pursue me to the water's edge; meanwhile
The scream grows worse – what the fuck is that?
It's like a knife right through me – and only water
Seems to offer some relief – respite from this litany
Terrible noise-clutter disturbance jangling cacophony
Of failure, horror, black despair, this life I'm holding
In my murderous hands, the betrayal, the lies,
The evening phone calls, the skulking in hotels –
Because of course I had to choose a man
Who'd never love me best. Who'd only ever
Leave me. Because, and here's the truth,
I'm not like the others; *happy* – well, it's over there
Eternally unreached, unreachable

Just say it –

I don't deserve, I don't deserve, I don't deserve –
Love or life – they're wasted on a fool like me.

And I wade out into the water – clear solution –
End the noise. We'll go together. Best thing all round.

MAB

Well I left you at the Ness and rowed back into Orford and a-
course they knew by then you'd gone, and knew also it was me.
So I got tied up, same as you, and they brung in the instruments,
but really there was no need I told 'em the story of how I cut
you free, why should I not?

I ent afeared, I says, whatever brung it quickest. But some of
the squit they talk –

You witch-girl, with no husband, snarl de Glanville, presiding
like he's Lord Almighty, do you couple with sea monsters?
Have you brought forth demon children? Has your womb been
a cauldron for the monsters we have seen about this coast? –
well, then, I spit my blood into his face, and won't say a word.

So the charge is witchcraft on top of treachery which means a-
burnin – but the Bishop he pipe up, thank God –

Should we not try her with the water test?

My chance to drown, cos I don't fancy cookin – take the sweet
soft drown me, any day, allus said so –

So when they bind me to the chair and hurl me in, my only
thought to the gawpers on the quay, is Devil take you all, I'm
gone, I'm going home, and will not be back to scorch –

But blow me the stupid wooden chair I'm tied on, that do bob
and bob and turn about, and I am gulping sea, then air, then sea
again, and wishing we could get this over – and the screaming
of the mob up on the quay clutters in my head a terrible
disturbance and I'm just longing for the quiet – and if only a
last look of you, my other half – but you are lost to me – lost for
evermore – returned to your element, that I know, but if there's
one thing in my life I cling to, it is that – that you are free – and
twas I that cut the rope and let you go –

When on a sudden these strong arms grasp my legs… strong
arms wrap around me… from beneath the waves… I have
bobbed far out now from the roaring quay and gawping mob,
I'm out towards the Ness, and these strong warm arms are
pulling at my legs, and drawing me under, the chair is sinking
down, the waves close over my head, I'm deep, I'm deep, I'm

under now, the noise clutter from the shore tunes out and I hear bells, and bells and pealing, and there's you, there's you, you draw me under, deep, so deep, far deeper than our depth and my hair billow out and flow and the ropes unloose and you are pulling on my legs to pull me under till the thrash and struggle's over and down I goo into the quiet – floatin –

BEN

And then I hit the water and man, it's like, I want to die, it's so cold, but it's kind of a good cold, the way it hurts so bad – and I go deeper and deeper till I stumble, lose my footing, then I'm swimming –

and all the time, the auroral disturbance, which for some reason I am still perceiving as screaming, it's peaking

And I wish I had some gear here I so I could prove it – Fuck you, Lindstrom, I found it, I saved the day!

...but if only it would stop, the fucking noise, it hurts my head, it feels like screaming – and I swim and swim to get away but the noise gets worse and I realise the auroral disturbance is in me and the current flings me and I'm half-breathing water and I know my body's going mad to save itself but my mind is strangely open

And flickering like a screen – there's Mike and me, Mike Tomiyoshi, laughing like we used to, old buddies, on a film looping and replaying and we're on the balloon, like everything is – and then remorse goes through me like nine hundred volts and the shock becomes words and the words are all I am: *forgive me*

and suddenly

it's quiet

utter peace

the noise has gone

no more sky above but water

and I'm going deep deep towards the soft seabed to sleep

Last thoughts like bedtime linger… Mabel… and the fishskin trousers… and I didn't say goodbye to Mum –

When a shape looms up toward me, underwater… like a Russian submarine except I don't have to care about that any more – and when I pirouette closer it seems to be… a body… drifting, like my own – but no –

Her eyes are open – I think, my God, it's Mabel, looks like her –

but she's drowning and I know I have to save her, I have to get her out of this, and I swirl across the seabed like an astronaut or seahorse and I float her where the gentle inland current will take her to the shore – and as she sweeps away I catch her face so sweet and it's so like Mabel's, only no, not Mabel's, more like mine – mine

I send her out – she swirls away – and she – last thing I see

Before the tide takes me

out beyond all boundaries

and deeper than my depth –

and I am

I and

Am

I

MOG

He shoved me out – he swam me to the shore and pushed –
I swear – I saw a face beneath the water, a man, a bit like me –
And maybe I was dreaming – or maybe dying – but
I saw his eyes, ecstatic, joyful, and his hands reached out
And pushed me from the water before the current turned,
And pulled him far away.

Half-drowned but still alive on the shores of Orford Ness –
I spy my rucksack and remember it's my birthday –
I've got a present – I forgot – the box
From little Grace, Year Five, the gift she made…
I fumble in my rucksack – as I muse on you,
Still safe inside, my dearest darling, little dot, my sweet –
And pull out Grace's box – and open it.
And there inside unfolds a shimmering
Flood of something, glinting, glittering
Pretty fishskin, fashioned into tiny trousers
They give off rainbows – perfect for a one-year-old
And I vow you'll wear them on your birthday, when it comes
And we celebrate the two of us, neither of us perfect
But neither of us more nor less guilty
Than any creature given
From the hand of life
Upside down
In water
At the centre
Of the universe

MAB

And down in the deep below, here we are in this beauteous
seabed and he hand me this pair of most beautiful trousers made
of fishskin to match his own and I can count the toes of all the
mermaids in notes of sounds and I can see the smell of conch in
all the colours that you never saw and the many-sided pearl it
be three hundred and forty-eight and I am in my element and I
am dancing to the band and flying through the centuries, and he
my other half say welcome and do hand me these breeches that
glint so pretty all the rainbow scales of pretty-coated fish and he
say to me he say, you must try them, Mab.

And I do.

The End.

TIME SPENT ON TRAINS

Time Spent on Trains was first performed at the Miniaturists, Southwark Playhouse, London, on 18 June 2006, with the following cast:

JENNY	Lindsey Bourne
PETER	Robert Price
Director	Elizabeth Kuti

Characters

JENNY

PETER

JENNY *is wearing floaty summer clothes, slightly reminiscent of 1977.*

PETER *is thirty-seven and wears a suit and tie. He has bare feet. He does not look at* JENNY, *ever.*

They are on a train.

An announcement comes over the tannoy.

ANNOUNCEMENT. British Rail regrets that this service has been delayed. Please await further announcements.

JENNY. Peter.
    Peter.
    Peter.
    Peter.
    Peter.
    Oh, Peter.
    Petey.
    Peets.
    Hey, Peets.
    I love you.
    I love you.
    Hey.
    Peter.

    Hey.

    This is such an adventure.
    I love going on adventures with you.
    I love trains.

PETER. Yes. Trains. Yes.

JENNY. When I was little, I mean when I was young, I had to get a train to school every day. Every single day. And the train we got always used to have those tiny little carriages which are just the two rows of seats facing each other, like a first-class compartment only without the corridor going down the side. We used to call them doggy-boxes.

Or a dog-box if you were cool.
Get us a dog-box, Jen!
Except I wasn't cool at all.
But when someone managed to get a doggy-box we'd climb
up and sit in the luggage racks and travel in style with our
bums parked right up high by the ceiling. And sometimes
we'd take out the light bulbs. So that when you went through
a tunnel it went completely pitch black. And there was this
really long tunnel just before we got to our stop that went on
for ever. Or several minutes anyway but that's a long time
when you're in a tunnel. Especially when it's so pitch black
you can't even see your – (*Holds her hand right in front of
her eyes.*) And you're rocking along up in the luggage rack
bold as brass seventy miles an hour in the pitch dark
screaming – that was the point of the whole thing – to
scream like lunatics right through the tunnel. Or stop and
listen to everyone else screaming.

And then they told us in assembly – never ever get into one
of those carriages beacuse something awful might happen.
And there was this rumour that something awful had
happened to somebody from fourth year in a dog-box, so we
kind of went off them. Nowhere to run, nowhere to hide. Just
you and the pervert. Probably wasn't true, anyway, probably
just our feverish imaginations.

Hey. Peter.
Who's this?

She does a very good Tyrannosaurus Rex impersonation.

Who am I?

Oh come on you know it, it's easy.

She does it again.

Well I think it's easy. It's all in the – (*Holds up two little two-
fingered claws.*) Tyrannosaurus – ?

Rex.
T. Rex.

Do you not want your shoes on, darling?
Are your feet not cold?

You look ever so smart.
Shoes?

PETER. I don't want.

JENNY. Okay.
No rush.
We're not going to be there for a while anyway.

God, look at the sky.
Could you be just a bit more blue please?
I love the sky.
Do you love the sky, Petey?
You may scoff but where'd we be without it? We'd be lost without it.
Be like going out without your hat.
Oh damn.
I think we're going to be late.
I should have rung at Colchester.
Wait four months for an appointment and then be late for the damn thing.
They'll just have to deal with it won't they?
They've kept us waiting long enough now they'll just have to wait for us.
Not our fault anyway, we got diverted.

PETER. Not our fault we got diverted.

JENNY. Our fault a bit, my fault, should have got an earlier one. But not your fault – definitely not your fault.

PETER. Definitely not your fault.

JENNY. That's very sweet of you, darling, but – They might beg to differ. I should have rung. Bugger.
Do you know what I wish?
I wish someone would invent a special magic telephone you could just carry around with you and whenever you were late you could just whip it out and go – 'Hello! Someone jumped on the track so the train got diverted so I'm going to be late and if you'd given us the bloody appointment in March like you said you were going to this probably wouldn't have happened would it? See you when we see you! Bye!'
Magic telephone. Brilliant idea. I always know exactly what

people ought to invent, I just can't –
I'd be a bloody genius if I was just a bit cleverer.

Do you not want your socks on at least?
Baby?
Aren't you a little bit cold?

Hey?

*She searches on the seat behind her and then holds out
towards him a very small child's pair of shoes and socks.*

Hey? What do you say? No?
Yes please?
Or no thank you?
No I don't want my socks!
Or yes I do! Yes I do! I want my socks please?
Which is it?
Yes please I want! Or no. No I don't want –

PETER. No. I don't want – I don't want –

JENNY. Right.
Okay but you'll have to when we get off okay? Is that a
deal? Okay? Do we have a deal?

PETER. Do we have a deal.

JENNY. Yes, we have a deal, okay. We have a deal. I might read
my book for a little bit is that all right? Is that all right?

PETER. Yes.

JENNY. I love reading on trains.

She gets out her book and starts reading.

PETER. She loves reading on trains. She loves adventures. We
love adventures. We are going to be late. There is a delay.
There is an unavoidable delay. We love to read on trains.
Someone jumped on the track. They called them a dog-box
and something awful happened. But perhaps it didn't perhaps
it was a feverish rumour. Magic telephone is a brilliant idea.
She is a genius. She. Rocking along with your bum parked
up high by the ceiling and scream scream scream –
I love the train. I love – flash flash flash flying. Rock a rock a

rock a rock a rock a rocka rocka
Whoooooooowhooooooooooh!

When I think of her we are on a train and there is this
unavoidable delay –
We are diverted.
We are late for the appointment.
But –

JENNY. Oh! Sheep! Look!
    Sheep! Petey!
    Oh!
    Baaa!

    Baaa!

PETER. There is this diversion. We are being diverted.
    Delayed. We spent a lot of time on trains being delayed.

JENNY. Did you see? Baa baa black sheep,
    Have you any…?

    Wool. Yes sir yes sir, three bags… – ?
    Three bags – ?

    Three bags – ?

    Three bags – ?

PETER (*tiny voice*). Fff –

JENNY. YES!!! YES!!! Three bags full! Three bags full!
    Fantastic! Great talking. One for the master and one for the
    dame and one for the – ?
    One for the – ?
    One for the little –

    Boy who lives down the lane.

    Would you like to read a book? Shall we read – What shall
    we read? How about – ah – oh God I forgot your book.

    But – I didn't forget it because I can remember it in my head.
    Ahmmm – da da da da – (*Trying to remember first line*.)

PETER. In my head. We are being diverted on an unavoidable
    delay beause somebody jumped, beause we are in the

dog-box, I am in the dog-box, it's not my fault but it is
dangerous so even now even now I like my – I like my
shoes off, so I feel, I feel like, the same – same as – all those
times, when she let me take them off, the times we were
always late for an appointment –

JENNY. Got it. Right.
On the night Max wore his wolf suit and was naughty in one
way or another his mother called him – ?

She does a little bit of the T. Rex impersonation.

Wild thing. And Max said I'll eat you all so he was sent to
bed without his supper. But then that night in Max's room a
forest grew and grew and grew until the walls became the
world all around and the waves tumbled by with a private
yacht for Max and he sailed away for a year and a day and
through a week and beyond a year to the land where the wild
things are and when he got to the land where the wild things
are – they roared their terrible roars and showed their terrible
claws but Max said – Max said –
Showed their terrible claws but Max said –
Remember the page? Page with all the monsters?
Max said – ?

Say it for me, baby.

You know this one. Make me happy.

PETER. So much time spent on trains going for appointments.
So many questions, questions, questions. I hate the sandpit
and I hate the glue but I love the slide. Good days, bad days.
She forgets my book. She loves reading her book but she
forgets my book.

JENNY. Make me happy. Say it for me.

PETER. In Max's room a forest grew and grew and grew until
the ceiling hung with vines –

JENNY. Did I get the words wrong? Is that it?

PETER. And the walls became the world all around –

JENNY. What did I do wrong?

PETER. Do wrong.

JENNY. Peter.
　　You said it yesterday, I know you know it.
　　Yesterday.
　　I heard you say it.
　　So look at me and say it.
　　Say it.
　　Look
　　At
　　Me.

PETER. Wild things roared their terrible roars and showed their
　　terrible claws but –

JENNY. But Max said – ?

PETER. When I was young, I mean when I was little, I went on
　　trains all the time, all the time, always so many
　　appointments.

JENNY. Because sometimes I just need you to say what you
　　said yesterday. I just need you to give me a sign. To connect
　　us. To say that you see the sky with me.

PETER. They had a sandpit and a slide and they had crisps if
　　you did the block right. I got the block right sometimes. I
　　was very teachable. They could teach me. I was teachable. I
　　got the crisps a lot. And now I am on trains a lot, sufficiently
　　high-functioning to be on a train. I go to the centre. There is
　　crisps. They said are you okay to be on the train alone and I
　　said, yes, I know about trains, I will never get into a dog-
　　box.
　　So
　　The walls became the world all around.

　　And they have magic telephones for real now.

　　She was right.
　　She was a genius.

JENNY *is in despair.*

Be still.

JENNY. Because the sky is so beautiful and you are so beautiful and you are part of all that is and I will not be afraid.

PETER. Be still.

JENNY. What?

PETER. Be still.

Pause.

JENNY. But Max said be still. And tamed them by looking into all their yellow eyes at once.

Pause. She recovers.

PETER. Sky.

JENNY (*with enormous relief and pleasure*). Sky. Yes. Yes, my darling. Sky.

She smiles happily as the train rocks on. They both look out of the window.

End.

ENTER A GENTLEMAN

Enter A Gentleman was first performed at the Miniaturists, Arcola Theatre, London, on 10 July 2011, with the following cast:

APHRA BEHN	Shanaya Rafaat
WILLMORE	Fred Gray
ANGELLICA	Eline Powell
JOHN HOYLE	Adam Jackson-Smith
Director	Robert Price

It was subsequently performed at the National Portrait Gallery, London, on 11 November 2011, with the following cast:

APHRA BEHN	Georgia Buchanan
WILLMORE	Marco Petrucco
ANGELLICA	Helen Matravers
JOHN HOYLE	Edward Walters
Director	Leon Rubin

Introduction

Over a period of nearly twenty years Aphra Behn wrote plays for the Restoration theatre, starting with *The Forced Marriage* in 1670, and finishing with *The Widow Ranter*, which was first produced posthumously in November 1689, a few months after her death. Her gift to the theatre was huge. Her significance for actresses, as well as for female playwrights, cannot be overestimated. She created some of the most brilliant roles for women in the canon of English drama, roles that were not to be matched for a good couple of hundred years.

The spur to write this play came from the collection of Behn's letters published after her death under the title *Love Letters to a Gentleman*. I had owned these for years but never read them until one day in 2011 when I sat in my kitchen and on an impulse opened the book. And I was immediately overwhelmed by the sheer energy and life that sang out from the pages. I found it impossible not to read them out loud, because the voice that spoke so urgently and passionately in them just demanded to be heard. Despite the masked identities – they are written to someone addressed as 'Lycidas' and signed 'Astrea' – this pastoral game-playing is the only aspect of them that could be seen as chintzy or effete. In all other ways they are alive with a raw energy: teasing, funny, self-mocking and playful; full of agonised wit, sexual yearning, tender and angry passion. The line between Aphra Behn's life and her fiction is notoriously blurry, and contested; but it seems impossible not to read these love letters as just that – the real thing, not fiction but the genuine record of a passionate love affair. Some Behn scholars (Duffy, Goreau, Todd, Hughes) have argued along these lines, and suggested that 'Astrea' of the letters is Aphra, and 'Lycidas' is John Hoyle, originally from York, the Puritan lawyer and son of the notorious regicide (and suicide) Thomas Hoyle. The love affair between Aphra Behn and John Hoyle documented in *Love Letters to a Gentleman*, is at the heart of this play.

The historical facts are these. John's father, Thomas Hoyle
hanged himself, apparently maddened and haunted by visions of
the king he had helped to behead (according to one source he
died in a state of distraction, crying out 'I am damned for the
blood of the King', Goreau). His son John Hoyle became a
lawyer at Gray's Inn. Despite their opposed political allegiances,
Aphra, among many others, became fascinated by Hoyle;
seemingly enthralled and appalled by him in equal measure. She
wrote many poems to him and about him, addressing him
sometimes as J.H. but often as Lysander, Amyntas or Lycidas. In
her poem *Our Cabal*, Behn describes Hoyle ensnaring the
affections of 'poor Doris and Lucinda too / And many more
whom thou dost know / Who had not the power his charms to
shun / Too late to find themselves undone.' Hoyle seems to have
been a deeply troubled and troubling person, a man of wit and
learning, but also violent, iconoclastic, emotionally manipulative,
and seemingly dangerously attractive to both sexes.

During his lifetime, Hoyle's numerous relationships with men
and women had brought him public notoriety; and had nearly
cost him his life. Sodomy was at this time a capital offence.
Documents discovered quite recently in 1994 by P.M. Hopkins
give new and fascinating details of the lawsuit brought against
Hoyle in 1686–7 by a poulterer's apprentice, a youth of about
seventeen, called Benjamin Bourne. This was some years after
the affair with Behn had ended:

> Mr Hoyle of the Temple a person of good abilityes and witt
> has Buggery sworne against him by a youth… the matter
> came on Wednesday to the King's bench (Mr Hoyle
> confessed some indecent familiarityes with the Boy, some
> say enough to hang himself)… Mr Hoyle is committed to
> prison to Newgate. It is too publickly known that Mr Hoyle
> 10 or 12 yeares since kept Mrs Beane – and that there was a
> difference between them two and that this boy used to carrey
> Messages between them but I suppose they two had
> interrupted all acquaintance many years since.

Hopkins points out that the relationship between Hoyle and
Behn clearly lingered long in the public memory if it had
occurred 'ten or twelve years' prior to this court case, and yet
was still 'publickly known'. This passage of time is consistent

with the speculation that Mrs Behn had indeed been Hoyle's 'kept mistress' ten or twelve years previously, in the years between late 1674 to early 1677. The intriguing story suggested by the document just quoted is that Benjamin Bourne, the eighteen-year-old poulterer's apprentice who accused Hoyle of 'indecent acts' in 1686, had as a lad of six or seven carried letters between Aphra Behn and John Hoyle during a stormy period in their love affair ten or twelve years earlier, at a time when they evidently had been conducting a rather public row or disagreement. Years later, as a young man, Benjamin Bourne seems to have succumbed to Hoyle's sexual demands, whether consensually or because of a financial arrangement we don't know. The only (evocative!) detail we do know is that Hoyle gave Bourne a pair of turtle doves, though whether this was a romantic gift or actual payment, we don't know. Whatever the true story was, the outcome was that the court case against Hoyle was dropped and a verdict of ignoramus was returned; Hoyle escaped the hangman's noose on that occasion.

Aphra died three years later in 1689; and it is believed that John Hoyle wrote the epitaph on Behn's tomb in Westminster Abbey – the tone of which is (not surprisingly, given its author) extremely ambiguous:

> Here lies a proof that wit can never be
> Proof against mortality.

Is this playful, ironic, nihilistic, acerbic, reproving? I'm not sure. And I'm not sure how pleased Aphra Behn would have been with it either.

Hoyle himself survived Aphra by three years, but eventually was murdered in 1692. He bled to death in the street of a stomach wound inflicted in the course of an alcohol-fuelled fight in The Young Devil Tavern in Fleet Street. He was around fifty years old. 'Mr Hoyle was an Atheist, a sodomite professed, a corrupter of youth and a blasphemer of Christ' was how Whitelock Bulstrode (who had once been Cromwell's chaplain) described him at the time of his death. It was a different age by then – the dominant Stuart ethos of excess and libertinism had, in the age of William and Mary, been replaced by the moralistic, bourgeois consensus that Behn had spent much of her life mocking and satirising.

However, back at the height of their affair in the early to mid-1670s, we find a repeated dynamic in the *Love Letters* – a power struggle in which Astrea (Aphra) berates Lycidas (Hoyle) for his coldness, which only inflames her desire the more. Her constant complaint is that Hoyle withholds his heart, keeping the upper hand in the relationship by refusing to return her passion with the same warmth. We are given evocative details of their lives; the letters examine with a lover's jealousy the minutiae of social behaviour, of perceived slights from the lover, and changes in the mood and temperature of the relationship: 'Why then did you say you would not sit near me? Was that, my friend, the esteem you profess? Who grows cold first? Who is changed? And who the aggressor? 'Tis I was first in friendship, and shall be last in constancy.' (Letter III) This is the game of love as war, in which Aphra Behn pleads for 'plain-dealing' from him, but fears that her own emotional openness means she is on the losing side:

> I assure you I do not, nor never did love, or talk at the rate I do to you, since I was born... If it be troublesome 'tis because I fancy you lessen whilst I increase in passion... my dear, faithless Lycidas... I conjure thee, if possible to come tomorrow about seven or eight at night, that I may tell you in what a deplorable condition you left me tonight. I cannot describe it; but I feel it, and with you the same pain, for going so inhumanely. But oh! You went to joys and left me to torments! You went to love alone, and left me love and rage, fevers and calentures, even madness itself! Indeed, indeed my soul! (Letter VII)

At other times she demands better treatment: 'I grow desperate fond of you and would fain be used well; if not, I will march off... come for God's sake betimes tomorrow and... do not shame me with your perpetual ill opinion; my nature is proud and insolent and cannot bear it; I will be used something better!' (Letter VI) In another mood she casts a mock-curse upon him for going to a dance without her: 'I cannot help wishing you no mirth,' she writes in a fit of jealousy, 'nor any content in your dancing design... May your women be all ugly, ill-natured, ill-dressed, ill-fashioned and unconversable; and for your greater disappointment may every moment of your time there be taken

up with thoughts of me.' Even if this period of the affair with
Hoyle is notable for the absence of productions of Behn's plays
in the theatre – he appeared to 'keep' her, thus perhaps lessening
the financial incentive to get her plays produced – nonetheless
she was continuing to write. Maureen Duffy proposes that in
this next letter she is discussing her new play *The Rover*:

> I stayed after thee tonight, till I had read a whole act of my
> new play; and then he led me over all the way saying, 'Gad,
> you were the man'… he said you were not handsome, and
> called 'Philly' to own it; but he did not, but was of my side,
> and said you were handsome.

The cryptic conversation referred to here, if it is about *The
Rover*, may be a discussion between Aphra Behn and Charles
Davenant or Thomas Betterton – both of whom lived in the
Davenant household in Dorset Street, 'over the way' from
Behn's lodgings. The chief participant in the discussion declares
'Gad you [i.e. Hoyle] were the man' – that is, the model for
Willmore, the eponymous hero of *The Rover*. This is followed
by a debate about whether or not 'you' (Hoyle) was handsome:
Behn and 'Philly' arguing yes, the chief disputant arguing no.
This is speculative. However, *The Rover, Part One*, was staged
in 1677, seemingly shortly after the break-up of the affair
between Behn and Hoyle. And it seems clear that Hoyle is, at
least partly, parodied and captured in Willmore, the Rover. It's a
mocking, affectionate, satirical portrait of Hoyle, and the breed
of Restoration libertine he typified (along with glances at
Rochester and Charles II himself perhaps). It's a portrait in
which Behn also depicts herself – or perhaps, her enraptured self
of a year or two earlier, at the height of the relationship with
Hoyle – in the character of Angellica Bianca, the courtesan.

Aphra Behn's identification with Angellica has been much
discussed. Suffice it to say that while other women in the play
see through Willmore ('to love such a shameroon, a very
beggar, nay a pirate beggar, whose business is to rifle and be
gone', says Moretta, Angellica's bawd), Angellica herself has
fallen painfully, helplessly in love – 'my heart!, my virgin heart,
Moretta! Oh 'tis gone!' The agonies of rejection and insecurity
that Angellica suffers closely resemble those of Aphra/Astrea of
the *Love Letters*:

He's gone and in this ague of my soul
The shivering fit returns;
Oh with what willing haste he took his leave,
As if the longed-for minute were arrived
Of some blessed assignation

Act 4, Scene 2

And later, Angellica's complaints to Willmore echo the
sentiments of the poetry: 'How many poor believing fools thou
hast undone? / How many hearts thou hast betrayed to ruin?'
(Act 5). Read alongside the *Love Letters*, Angellica Bianca's
passion for Willmore seems barely fictional but absolutely
drawn from Behn's life; and even the plotting of the play in
which there is a young 'boy' – or rather, the young heroine
Hellena in disguise as a page – is resonant with what we know
of Behn and Hoyle's affair, and their go-between, the letter-
deliverer and messenger-boy, Benjamin Bourne. As we have
seen, Bourne later became Hoyle's lover – just as Hellena wins
Willmore from Angellica at the end of *The Rover, Part One*.

Which brings us to actresses. In *The Rover, Part One*, Angellica
Bianca was played by Anne Quin, while Elizabeth Barry played
the part of Hellena, the witty virgin and heiress. However, in the
sequel, *The Rover, Part Two*, first produced in 1681, Elizabeth
Barry took over the part of the Angellica character, in this play
called La Nuche. If in *The Rover, Part One*, Angellica Bianca
commanded unexpected sympathy as the passionate but
abandoned mistress, who cannot bring herself to kill Willmore
despite her rage at his treatment of her, in *The Rover, Part Two*
we see a fantasy of healing and reconciliation between the
Rover and his courtesan mistress. La Nuche tells the Rover: 'I
was told that if this night I lost you, I shou'd never regain you:
now I am yours, and o're the Habitable World will follow you,
and live and starve by turns as fortune pleases' to which he
replies 'give me thy hand, no poverty shall part us – so – now
here's a bargain made without the formal foppery of Marriage'
(Act 5). Elizabeth Barry was so acclaimed as La Nuche that in
future productions of *The Rover, Part One* she took over the
part of Angellica Bianca, a role she played for the next thirty
years. The critic Elizabeth Howe has argued that Elizabeth
Barry's talent in this role and others like it led to 'an interesting

shift in focus away from the traditional heroine onto the suffering mistress, who became the most important character in the play' and that 'it was only when Barry's mesmeric talents were employed in the portrayal of prostitutes and mistresses that their problematic situation was given detailed consideration and their sufferings vividly realised... Aphra Behn and other comic dramatists went on to create more variations on the suffering mistress for Barry to play' (Howe). The relationship between Elizabeth Barry and Aphra Behn was many-layered, encompassing friendship, love and professional collaboration – 'Mrs Barry was to have a part – often a leading role – in almost every play Aphra Behn wrote for the rest of her career' (Goreau). It was a partnership which Howe has argued profoundly affected dramatic literature, instigating a generic shift towards 'she-tragedy' and an interest in the 'suffering' woman or abandoned mistress, not as a figure of fun or an object of pity – not as an object at all – but as a human character of intense emotional and dramatic interest.

If the arrival of the actress created and enabled the female playwright, the female playwright also created and empowered the actress. Their collaboration meant that lived female experience could be transmuted into art on the English stage. And, furthermore, the arrival of the female playwright also created a new era in terms of the representation of men; the woman dramatist could create portraits of men and male characters 'from the outside', allowing new levels of critical insight, affection and understanding. The actress and the female playwright arrive together in the 1660s in the English theatre; and they bring with them a whole new version of the male character: the male as object, viewed from the outside – viewed, for the first time, objectively. For this reason, among others, I have called this play, *Enter A Gentleman*.

References

Behn, Aphra. *Love Letters to a Gentleman* and *The Rover* in *Oroonoko, The Rover and Other Works* edited by Janet Todd (Harmondsworth: Penguin, 1992); and *The Rover, Part Two* in *The Complete Works of Aphra Behn,* 7 volumes, edited by Janet Todd (London: Pickering, 1992)

Duffy, Maureen. *The Passionate Shepherdess: Aphra Behn, 1640–89* (London: Cape, 1977)

Goreau, Angeline. *Reconstructing Aphra: a social biography of Aphra Behn* (New York: Dial Press, 1980)

Hopkins, P.A. 'Aphra Behn and John Hoyle: A contemporary mention and Sir Charles Sedley's poems on his death', *Notes and Queries* (June 1994)

Howe, Elizabeth. *The First English Actresses: Women and Drama, 1660–1700.* (Cambridge University Press, 1992)

Hughes, Derek. *The Theatre of Aphra Behn.* (Palgrave, 2001)

Todd, Janet. (ed.) *Aphra Behn.* (Palgrave Macmillan, 1999); and (ed.) *The Cambridge Companion to Aphra Behn* (Cambridge University Press, 2004)

Characters

APHRA BEHN

WILLMORE

ANGELLICA

JOHN HOYLE

Bare stage.

Lights up on APHRA BEHN, *holding a script. She is in the theatre, rehearsing her new play,* The Rover, *onstage.*

APHRA. Enter a Gentleman.

An actor playing WILLMORE *enters in cavalier fashion, holding a scroll of paper.*

In an Undress. He has come from a Debauch.

In an Undress?

WILLMORE *removes some clothing and musses up his hair.*

Thank you.

WILLMORE. This can be none but my pretty gipsy –

APHRA. The Lady must enter first.

WILLMORE. Sorry.

APHRA. Enter Angellica in a masquing habit and a vizard.

Enter ANGELLICA *in a masquing habit and vizard, also with a scroll of paper.*

This can be none –

WILLMORE. This can be none but my pretty gipsy – So do I – ?

APHRA. Willmore runs to her.

WILLMORE *runs to her.*

ANGELLICA. Stand off, base villain.

WILLMORE. Hah, 'tis not she, who art thou? And what's thy business?

ANGELLICA. One thou hast injured, and who comes to kill thee for't.

WILLMORE. What the devil canst thou mean?

ANGELLICA. By all my hopes to kill thee.

WILLMORE. Prithee, on what acquaintance? For I know thee not.

ANGELLICA. Madam, it seems to me that she needs to –

APHRA. Yes, that's right, so here – 'on what acquaintance? I know thee not' – the vizard comes off – and when she says 'Behold this face' et cetera he finally recognises –

ANGELLICA. No, yes, I see, but I wondered –

WILLMORE. It's not your job to wonder, darling.

ANGELLICA. She's threatening to kill him –

WILLMORE. But not in earnest.

APHRA *and* ANGELLICA. She is in earnest!

ANGELLICA. That's what I thought!

WILLMORE. Not at this point, surely? It's only later when he offers her the money that she really seems to –

ANGELLICA. I think she means to kill him. From the very beginning. She has come to kill him, she says so – 'One who comes to kill thee for't.'

APHRA. Yes. He's broken her heart, quite deliberately. She means to kill him.

ANGELLICA. Then what is she intending to use? Shouldn't she have something in her hand – a knife or a – ? a poniard? I mean, do we know, have we decided?

APHRA. A dagger? Do we have a dagger?

WILLMORE. I don't like working with daggers. We've had some very nasty –

ANGELLICA. So that when she says 'stand off, base villain' she can actually –

APHRA. Get something out – and – yes, that's good, that's better –

ANGELLICA. Stand off!

APHRA. Yes!

ANGELLICA. Because he's armed, he has a weapon –

APHRA. Yes!

ANGELLICA. So she needs to have a –

APHRA. Yes, so, ah, what if – (*Delves around beneath her skirts – pulls out a small knife.*)

APHRA. Do you think…?

ANGELLICA *tries it out.*

ANGELLICA. Stand off, base villain!

WILLMORE *draws his sword.*

What do you think?

APHRA. It's not really working.

WILLMORE. I think it reads quite well.

ANGELLICA. No, she needs something more…

APHRA. It's not working. She needs –

APHRA *pulls a small jewelled pistol from her bodice.*

More like this?

ANGELLICA. May I?

Could we?

She enters, 'My pretty gipsy', he runs to her and –

(*Draws pistol and threatens.*) Stand off, base villain!

WILLMORE. Hah! – 'tis not she, who art thou? And what's thy business?

ANGELLICA. One thou hast injured, and who comes to kill thee for't.

WILLMORE. What the devil canst thou mean?

ANGELLICA. By all my hopes to kill thee.

APHRA. Yes!

WILLMORE. A little too much. To my mind.

APHRA. No, It's really more –

ANGELLICA. I feel much more – *there* – with this –

WILLMORE. The dynamic is completely –

APHRA. It works really well –

ANGELLICA. Can we – ?

APHRA. Yes. Keep going. 'Prithee on what'…?

WILLMORE. Prithee, on what acquaintance? For I know thee not.

ANGELLICA (*takes off vizard*). Behold this face! – so lost to thy remembrance,
And then call thy sins about thy soul,
And let 'em die with thee.

WILLMORE. Angellica!

APHRA. Good –

ANGELLICA. Yes, traitor,
Does not thy guilty blood run shivering through thy veins?
Hast thou no horror at this sight, that tells thee
Thou hast not long to boast thy shameful conquest?

WILLMORE. Faith, no child, my blood keeps its old ebbs and flows still, and that usual heat too, that could oblige thee with a kindness, had I but opportunity.

ANGELLICA. Devil! Dost wanton with my pain – have at thy heart.

WILLMORE. By heaven, thou'rt brave and I admire thee strangely.
To gain your credit, I'll pay you back your charity,
And be obliged for nothing but for love.

He offers her a purse of gold. Sorry, I don't seem to have –

APHRA *pulls out a purse and gives it to him.*

Thank you… da da da be obliged for nothing but for love.
Offers the purse of gold.

You see, I think this is the moment where she really –

ANGELLICA. I've heard thee talk too long –

WILLMORE. Sure –

ANGELLICA. Another word will damn thee!
   Now, for the public safety of my sex –
   And for my own private injuries –
   To show my utmost of contempt –

   Is there a line missing?

   There's a blank here.

   Or do you mean this is where she –

   To show my utmost of contempt –

   (*Mimes firing gun.*) BANG!

   WILLMORE *fails to react.*

WILLMORE. Sorry?

ANGELLICA. Now for the public safety of my sex
   And for my own private injuries –
   To show my utmost of contempt –

   BANG!

WILLMORE. Oh, right, sorry.

   He dies, and slumps down dead.

ANGELLICA. Something like that?

APHRA. Yes. That was very good.

WILLMORE. I don't believe it.

ANGELLICA. It's not your job to believe it, darling, it's your
   job to make them believe it.

WILLMORE. She wouldn't be able to do it. She loves him.

APHRA. If I say she does it then she does it.

WILLMORE. Madam, your forte is comedy. That's all I would say.

ANGELLICA. We need her to win. The audience needs her to win.

WILLMORE. If Willmore dies he becomes a tragic hero.

ANGELLICA. Hardly.

WILLMORE. If that's what you want then…

APHRA. Could I see it again?

WILLMORE. From the top?

APHRA. Please.

WILLMORE *and* ANGELLICA *leave the stage.*

Thank you.

Enter a Gentleman.

In an Undress.

Enter JOHN HOYLE, *half-dressed.*

The lights have shifted. APHRA*'s thoughts are wandering.*

He has come from a Debauch.

JOHN. All this endless scribbling. (*Takes the script from her.*) Do something real for once.

APHRA. When I do that, I lose. On paper, I win. Every time.

JOHN. That's why it's no good.

APHRA. What do you mean?

JOHN. Winners are so boring. We get that story all the time. Triumph, victory, conquest… so deucedly tedious. Who wants to watch that?

APHRA. I thought conquest was quite up your street.

JOHN. In life, yes. In art, give me catastrophe and failure every time.

APHRA. Thank you for your advice.

JOHN. You are welcome.

APHRA. Come back to bed.

JOHN. I'm afraid I can't. I'm a little spent.

APHRA. Disappointing. Betimes tomorrow then?

JOHN. Tomorrow, I'm afraid, is no good.

APHRA. Friday?

JOHN. Friday is a little…

APHRA. I conjure you to come on Friday.

JOHN *laughs*.

Well I am engaged to dine on Saturday. So it cannot be then.
There is an entertainment on purpose for me.

JOHN. You will not miss me then. Farewell, sweet.

APHRA. I miss you always. And even when you're here I feel
the pain of your departure. I can never be happy. Next week?

JOHN. I'll be quick about my going, then, and shorten your
torment.

APHRA. Oh God, I knew, I knew it, I was told that if I lost you
tonight I would never regain you.

JOHN. Who told you that?

APHRA. Nobody. My heart. I have fooled myself into an
undoing.

JOHN. Dear Aphra. You were so sweet.

APHRA. Don't move. Stay here. Stay and we'll be happy.

JOHN. I cannot.

APHRA. You can. I know how to be happy. I will make so
much happiness and feed it all to you.

Damn it, I am smitten, I am smitten so heart-deep and it was
you, it was you – you dealt the blow and now you walk
away –

JOHN. Adieu.

APHRA. I take it back. I know your kind, I will drive you away with love, so I must keep you with spurning.

Begone then.

Get thee gone.

You dog, I must whip you to keep you loyal. Get out!

JOHN. That's the spirit.

APHRA. I hate thee.

JOHN. Oh hatred now, the very thing to rouse the edge of my desire.

APHRA. You perverse and wicked man, you feast on torments –

JOHN. I feast on love.

APHRA. Only to hunger the next morning for fresh meat.

JOHN. Forgive me. It's in my nature.

APHRA. To tire so fast of conquests?

JOHN. Lay siege, prevail, possess, move on. It's in my nature.

APHRA. That's a poor excuse! You choose your nature as it suits you. And the bloody trail you leave in your wake?

JOHN. The concern of women and surgeons.

APHRA. You owe me more.

JOHN. I owe you nothing.

APHRA. You are so unreasonable, you would have me pay, you would have me give, and you like a miser, would distribute nothing.

JOHN. Love don't keep accounts.

APHRA. If not love, then what of my purse – What of my four hundred crowns? The bail that saved your neck!

JOHN. Did I not repay you? The thousand times you died in my arms! The thousand kisses! What of those?

APHRA. I did not know I bought them!

JOHN. So you want repayment?

APHRA. With interest!

JOHN. I hate a whore that asks me money!

APHRA. And so do I!

JOHN. I accepted your help as a gift of love.

APHRA. I love you not, I need you not, I never did.

JOHN. You're lying.

APHRA. My heart is free from all disturbance.

JOHN. God hates a liar.

APHRA. Good. Then I am well beloved by God. I love you not.

JOHN. I beg to differ.

APHRA. Oh do you? Where's your proof?

JOHN. Your eyes brimful of dying lying love. Panting, heaving, sighing, oh, oh, John, oh, John –

APHRA. Then the greater shame must be yours to have proven on so many occasions such a grave disappointment.

JOHN. If you coerce an unwilling lover then you must be prepared for such disappointments.

APHRA. Unwilling?

JOHN. Tired. Perhaps.

APHRA. Coerce? By what means?

JOHN. Bribery, then, let us say.

APHRA. What bribe?

JOHN. Your too-much-open purse. Don't pretend, Madam, you don't know what vulnerabilities of mine you have exploited –

APHRA. Vulnerabilities?

JOHN. – what arts of persuasion you have used to get me to your chamber. I will not deny that exigency, at times, has led me here. Of course not every time.

APHRA. Oh so you have not come for money every time.

JOHN. That would be obscene.

APHRA. You have rarely come at all, in fact.

JOHN. I come when I can.

APHRA. You save it for your page.

JOHN. On that charge – I was acquitted. As you very well know. The boy was lying.

APHRA. Lying where? On your bed? The floor? The stable?

JOHN. Madam. I got off!

APHRA. Of course. You always do with boys involved!

JOHN. As you well know the grand jury returned a verdict of Ignoramus.

APHRA. You risk your neck to get inside a little beggarly apprentice of seventeen. John. A poulterer's boy that stinks of the hen-house.

JOHN. And what pray, Madam, does your house stink of?

APHRA. Of you. I sleep with your smell in my nostrils.

JOHN. He was as fragrant as a wench of fifteen newly washed in the pearly dew of a May Day morning. And he withdrew all charges.

APHRA. Because you gave him a pair of turtle doves.

JOHN. He was appreciative of poultry. It was a professional interest.

APHRA. I have finished with you. Our connection is over.

JOHN. No. It's not.

APHRA. Your dominion over my heart has ended.

JOHN. I'll wager it has not.

APHRA. I'll kill you to prove it. I will laugh and dance on your gravestone.

JOHN. And I will write your epitaph.

APHRA. All the wit in the world cannot keep you from the tomb!

JOHN. Aye. That'll do. But I'll rewrite it. You deserve a gravestone that scans.

APHRA pulls out her knife.

JOHN laughs.

Now this I like.

APHRA. Don't play the wanton lest I am tempted to end thy career before I end thy life.

JOHN. I'll make it easy for you. Here. My heart. My throat. What pleases you most?

APHRA. To see you squeal like a stuck pig when I put it in.

JOHN. Lady. I know the feeling. Do it, please, now, do it. Do it.

She wants to kill him.

She can't bring herself to kill him.

She throws the knife away.

APHRA. Here's failure enough to keep you happy. I hate the world too much without thee in it.

JOHN. By Heaven thou art brave and I do admire thee strangely.

APHRA. I give thee life. I give thee life.

Exit JOHN.

I give thee life.

APHRA starts writing.

Enter a Gentleman. In an Undress.

Enter WILLMORE, followed a moment later by ANGELLICA.

WILLMORE. This can be none but my pretty gipsy!

ANGELLICA. Stand off, base villain!

WILLMORE. Hah! 'Tis not she, who art thou?

And what's thy business?

ANGELLICA. One thou hast injured and who comes to kill thee for't.

APHRA *has been writing busily through all this.*

WILLMORE. Carrying on?

APHRA. No. I want to see the ending – 'Another word will damn thee!'

ANGELLICA. Another word will damn thee!
Now for the public safety of my sex
And for my own private injuries
To show my utmost of contempt –

APHRA *stops writing and gives her a new piece of paper.*

APHRA. Try this.

ANGELLICA. – To show my utmost of contempt –
I give thee life!
I give thee life – which if thou wouldst preserve,
Live where my eyes may never see thee more,
Live to undo someone, whose soul may prove
So bravely constant to revenge my love.

Madam – can I say? I don't like it. She would kill him! He has undone her utterly and ruined her and stolen her money and yet you allow him to leave! To love another and again, and win a fortune! The ladies will damn you for it.

WILLMORE. It's marvellous, darling, you know nothing of art. The affecting catastrophe – the horrible victory – it's perfect.

ANGELLICA. I am sorely disappointed.

Exit ANGELLICA.

WILLMORE. Bravo. I give thee life! Quite perfect. If I may say so, Madam, this could be your triumph.

By the way – are you happy with what I'm doing?

APHRA *picks up* JOHN*'s hat, which he has left behind on the stage. She puts it on* WILLMORE.

APHRA. Yes. Very happy.

The End.

Love Armed

Love in fantastic triumph sat,
Whilst bleeding hearts around him flowed,
For whom fresh pains he did create,
And strange tyrannic power he showed.
From thy bright eyes he took his fire,
Which round about in sport he hurled;
But 'twas from mine, he took desire,
Enough to undo the amorous world.

From me he took his sighs and tears,
From thee his pride and cruelty;
From me his languishments and fears,
And every killing dart from thee;
Thus thou and I the god have armed,
And set him up a deity;
But my poor heart alone is harmed,
Whilst thou the victor is, and free.

Aphra Behn, 1677

A Nick Hern Book

Fishskin Trousers first published in Great Britain in 2013 as a paperback original by Nick Hern Books Limited, The Glasshouse, 49a Goldhawk Road, London W12 8QP

Reprinted with a new cover in 2017

Fishskin Trousers copyright © 2013 Elizabeth Kuti
Time Spent on Trains copyright © 2013 Elizabeth Kuti
Enter A Gentleman copyright © 2013 Elizabeth Kuti

Elizabeth Kuti has asserted her right to be identified as the author of this work

Cover image: Rebecca Pitt

Designed and typeset by Nick Hern Books, London
Printed in Great Britain by Mimeo Ltd, Huntingdon, Cambridgeshire PE29 6XX

A CIP catalogue record for this book is available from the British Library

ISBN 978 1 84842 362 6